This book is dedicated
to our four favourite recipes.

Jordan, Alia, Tate and Max

Donna & Sean
xxx

愛

FOOD IS LOVE
by Sean & Donna Slack

Copyright @ 2021. All Rights Reserved.
First published in New Zealand by Art + Realism © 2021
artandrealism.com *by Jacquie Burke*

ISBN
Hardcover 9780473573447
ePub 9780473562663

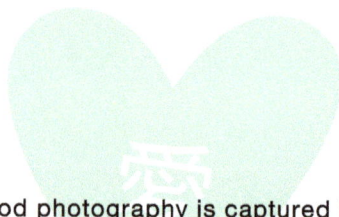

All amateur food photography is captured by Donna, Sean, and the Slack family as they go about their daily meals. In some cases, the natural light is not great - but that is feeding time at the Zoo! Hopefully, most parents can relate. Original cover photo by Jodie Morgan @twoluckyspoons. No food was wasted while making this book, everything was savoured and devoured, mouthful by mouthful. Made in New Zealand with love.

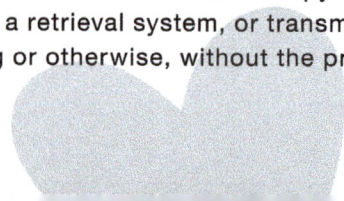

FOOD IS LOVE 愛

愛 EASY & DELICIOUS RECIPES FOR
THE MODERN FUSION FAMILY

by Sean & Donna Slack

OUR L**愛**VE STORY

We think the true love story began in 1999 when Sean invited Donna over to dinner and casually asked her to help.

Donna had never eaten, let alone made any of the food Sean was preparing and it turns out this was the first of many great collaborations they have embarked on over the years.

You may have heard the saying "the way to a man's heart is through his stomach", well it turns out that it works the same for women.

The Slacks

FOOD IS LOVE

To my four wonderful kids,

What I've realised is when it comes down to it, food is at the heart of everything. Food gives life, so for me, there's no greater act of love than feeding my family. Every mouthful means - I love you. It took me a long time to understand that part of Chinese culture. Food is how we say, I love you.

Turns out that's just as true if you're Maori, or Japanese or Italian, or Croatian; the family meal is the centre of everything.

So, passing on the food of my childhood that became the food of your childhood and will one day be the food of your adulthood, isn't meant as a gift. It's a necessity, as important as knowing how to read, write or cross the road. Every independent adult needs to be able to feed themselves; to cook something simple and delicious for themselves and the people they care about.

I hope these recipes remain part of the fabric of your life, sustain you, and remind you of the meals we have shared. They still have that power for me. Nothing connects me more strongly to my Mum than cooking her meals for us.

Never forget, food is love.
Dad

RECIPE INDEX *by Sean & Donna Slack*

START HERE
- Pantry Staples
- Bok Choy and Rice - *How to cook bok choy and make the perfect rice*

SAUCES & MAYO'S
- Chimmi Churri
- Nuoc Cham
- Ginger Spring Onion Sauce
- Japanese Sesame Mayo
- Sriracha Mayo

EASY SALADS
- Shamila's Mango Salad
- Donna's Japanese Coleslaw
- Donna's Prawn Cocktail Salad
- Thai Chicken Cucumber Salad

ASIAN INFLUENCED MEALS
- BBQ Pork
- Cantonese Braised Brisket
- Cantonese Steamed Fish
- Char Kway Teow *(Hawker Style Noodles)*
- Chilli Chicken Wings
- Chinese Red Cooked Pork
- Chicken Rice *(Hainanese)*
- Teriyaki Chicken
- Māmā's Siu Gai *(Chinese Roast Chicken)*
- Māmā's She-Yao Gai *(Soy Chicken)*
- Sweet 'n' Sour Pork
- Thai-style Deep Fried Fish
- Vietnamese Style Fried Pork
- Beef Bulgogi
- Vietnamese BBQ

WESTERN STYLE MEALS
- Fluffy Scrambled Eggs
- Slack Burgers
- Bacon Pesto Pasta
- Mum's Oxtail
- American BBQ Spare Ribs
- Donna's Roast Chicken *(Mediterranean)*
- Tate's Roaspie Chicken
- Sean's Macaroni Cheese
- Salmon Hash
- Mum's Xmas Turkey
- Xmas Pizza

SWEETS & TREATS
- Banana Bread
- Nan's Chocolate Rumble
- Nan's Feijoa Crumble

When you have these pantry staples all you have to do is buy the veges and the protein. If you've run out they're generally not too expensive to replace.

PANTRY STAPLES

Here is a list of pantry staples we think are a great starting point to make most of these tasty recipes.

RICE
Long grain

FROM THE PANTRY
Sugar
Butter
Chinese rice wine
Cooking sake
Rice wine vinegar
Sushi vinegar
Chinese five spice (packet)
Fish sauce
Mirin

Sesame seeds
Corn flour
Salt & pepper
Light soy sauce
Dark soy sauce
Kecap manis - Ketchup Asian style
Japanese mayonnaise (Kewpie)
Sriracha

COOKING OILS
Coconut oil
Rice bran oil
Olive oil

Grapeseed oil
Sesame oil

NB: Coconut oil, unlike other oils, can heat to a higher temperature and has a lovely subtle flavour which makes it great for cooking. Rice bran, canola, grapeseed are good, but they heat faster and can burn.

WATER
In our home, we have a large 20 litre water filter that removes chemicals, other impurities and mineralises the water. It really makes a difference to the over-all flavour of the food.

GET CREATIVE
When cooking, we rarely use correct measurements. We often make things up or try something a bit different. Feel free to add more, or less of something. If you don't have the right ingredients, you can always improvise.

PERFECT BOK CHOY + RICE

BOK CHOY

Wash and chop the ends off the bok choy. We recommend cutting the big leaves in half and keeping the small ones together. Smash a couple of garlic cloves and pop these into a bowl with the choy, white stems down.

Pour boiling water around the base of the leaves to steep for a couple of minutes. Heat a pan with coconut or rice bran oil.

Empty out most of the water. When the pan starts to smoke toss the bok choy into the pan and keep it moving, when the leaves start to wilt pour a little of the steeped water into the pan and cover quickly with a lid. Let it steam until all of the dark leaves are wilted, about a minute. Turn off the gas. Uncover and give it a toss to properly coat with oil.

Place the bok choy on a plate and pour a small amount of oyster sauce over it.

Additionally, roasted dried shallots sprinkled on top is extra delicious.

RICE

You need about 1 cup of uncooked rice for two people.

In the rice cooker rinse the rice 3-4 times to remove starch and dust. Do this until the water is clear.

Cover the rice with water and an extra 2cm or 1x finger joint. Switch it on and cook for 12-15 minutes.

Tip: If you don't have a rice cooker, once you've rinsed the rice in a pot, cover with water and boil on high until the water is barely visible then switch to the lowest setting. Put the lid on for approximately 2 minutes to finish steaming. Test it to check if it is cooked. If it's still a little crunchy, pop the lid back on for another minute or two and let it steam. It should be fluffy and not crunchy or sticky.

PREP TIME
5 minutes

COOK TIME
12-15 minutes

Once you have these two sussed you will never starve! - *Sean*

SAUCES

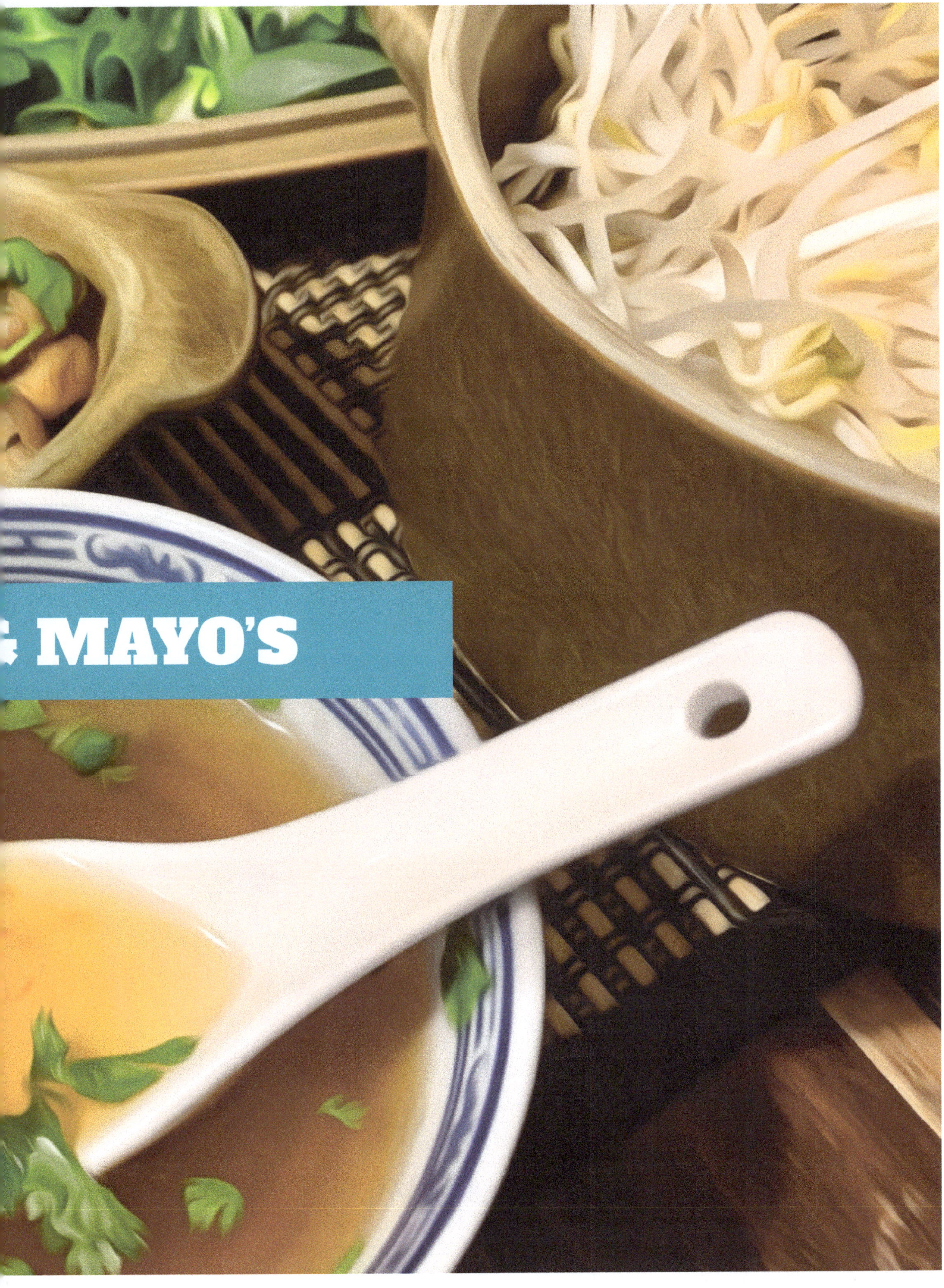
& MAYO'S

I spent 40 years not liking BBQ's.
This was the first summer
I loved it - thanks to our
chimichurri sauce - *Sean*

OUR CHIMICHURRI SAUCE

INGREDIENTS

1 cup extra virgin olive oil
2 tbsp lemon juice
2 tbsp red wine vinegar
1 small handful oregano leaves
3 large handfuls parsley
1 small handful corriander
¼ red onion

½ tsp ground black pepper
2 tsp sea salt
5 cloves garlic

METHOD

Finely chop all herbs and place in a bowl.

Crush and finely chop the garlic. Add the olive oil, salt, and pepper and mix.

Add finely chopped onion, vinegar, lemon juice and stir to combine. It's best if you cover and stand this for at least an hour, so it infuses.

Use it like this if you like it chunky but I prefer to put everything in a blender, briefly whizz and use straight away.

I've made this without the onion, coriander and lemon juice and it's just as good. I've also substituted the red onion for spring onion and if you like a little heat add a small (½ tsp) amount of finely chopped red chilli.

Tip: A handful of herbs equates to approximately 1 cup of leaves. Also, consider making extra because you can use it with many dishes. It keeps in the fridge for at least a week. Use a clean spoon each time you serve it and it won't get contaminated and go mouldy.

PREP TIME	COOK TIME	SERVES
15 minutes	0	Many

NUOC CHAM

VIETNAMESE DIPPING SAUCE

INGREDIENTS

¼ cup fish sauce
½ cup water
2 tbsp palm or raw sugar
2 tbsp lime juice
2 cloves chopped garlic
¼ cup rice vinegar

METHOD

Combine fish sauce, vinegar and water in a pot.

Heat and add sugar. Simmer (don't boil) until the sugar dissolves. Let it cool, then add the other ingredients.

You can jazz it up with some crushed pineapple (Vietnam cafe style) or chopped coriander. Or spice it up with a few finely chopped chillies.

Tip 1: We often use the Chinese ceramic soup spoon (pictured) as the equivalent of a tablespoon.

Tip 2: If you're using palm sugar, crush it in a mortar and pestle so it's easier to dissolve.

PREP TIME
15 minutes

COOK TIME
5 minutes

SERVES
Family of 6

Figured this out all by myself - *Sean*

I'm refining this every time I make it. I think it's called keung yook, but sheesh who knows. - *Donna*

GINGER SPRING ONION SAUCE

INGREDIENTS

3-4 whole spring onions
Approx ½ cup grated ginger
1 tsp salt
Rice bran oil to cover

METHOD

Chop the spring onions finely and pop into a bowl and cover with oil. Add approximately 1 teaspoon (15ml) of salt.

Finely grate the ginger and match the same amount of spring onion if you can. It seems like a lot but this is what makes it!

Add more oil to keep it covered, stir together. When it settles make sure there's at least 1 millimetre of oil on top.

If you leave it to sit for 15 minutes before use, it's even better and it will store well for weeks in the fridge (if you use a clean spoon each time you use it).

Excellent condiment to go with pork, chicken, fish and beef.

Tip: Seems like blasphemy, but when we are lazy we pop all ingredients into the food processor for a quick whizz. The colour is amazing when you do it this way. Sometimes we add some coriander stalks too. It gives it a fresh, zesty flavour.

PREP TIME
10 minutes

COOK TIME
0

SERVES
Many

JAPANESE SESAME MAYO

INGREDIENTS

3 tbsp white sesame seeds
2-3 tbsp mirin
1 tbsp light soy sauce
2 tsp raw sugar
1 tsp sesame oil
¼ cup of Japanese mayonnaise (Kewpie)

METHOD

Toast the sesame seeds in a dry pan until golden brown. Grind to a chunky powder in a mortar and pestle. The kids love doing this bit, the seeds pop as you grind them and it smells awesome. Don't grind the seeds too much, you want a few whole seeds in the sauce - it adds great texture.

Mix all ingredients together in a jar and shake it. If you don't have a jar, whisk the ingredients in a bowl.

Have a quick taste test, add a little more of the above ingredients to your preference.

Note: Light soy is thin and salty, dark soy is thicker and a little sweet, kecap manis is also a type of soy that is syrupy and sweeter still.

Tip: If you like the flavour to be richer and have some miso soup paste handy, add 1 teaspoon to the mix. A friend of ours has used maple syrup instead of sugar and said it was delicious. It also made it sugar free.

PREP TIME	COOK TIME	SERVES
15 minutes	*2 minutes*	*Many*

A must have with coleslaw
or Karaage chicken and works well with
anything Japanese, panko crumbed,
chicken or seafood - *Donna*

Excellent with fried chicken
or prawn salad! I felt very clever
getting this one right - *Donna*

SRIRACHA MAYO

INGREDIENTS

¼ cup Japanese mayonnaise (Kewpie)
1-2 tsp Sriracha chilli sauce
1 tsp American mustard

METHOD

Use a fork to mix all ingredients together in a small bowl.

Taste test to see if it needs more of one or the other.

I usually have to make twice the amount, especially if we're eating karaage.

Tip 1: Depending on how you feel, or what you're eating with this, you can swap the Sriracha and Mustard volumes. The Sriracha is warm and sweet and the Mustard makes it a little sour and tangy.

Tip 2: Kewpie mayo is thick and quite savoury compared to regular mayonaise. It's a little salty and we use it in everything. If you don't have Kewpie mayo, the next best thing is Best Mayonnaise. If you have neither - don't make it.

PREP TIME	COOK TIME	SERVES
1 minute	*0*	*Those who love it*

EASY DELIC

US SALADS

SHARMILA'S MANGO SALAD

INGREDIENTS

1 bag baby rocket
2 oranges - 6 thin slices and juice
½ red onion thinly sliced
1 half ripe firm mango sliced
Salt & pepper
Olive oil, drizzle

METHOD

Empty the bag of rocket into a bowl and remove the yellow and dead leaves.
Try not to wash it - it holds too much water. If you do wash it, use a salad spinner
to dry it well.

Cut 6 thin slices of orange, put aside to add to the salad. Squeeze and juice the
remaining orange into a small bowl and put aside. Peel and slice mango into bite
sized pieces.

Peel and slice the red onion and place into a glass and cover with cold water. Leave
for about 30 seconds, then pour off the water (this removes the burn from the onion).

Take a big wide bowl and put all ingredients together, toss with your hands so it
looks pretty. Put it aside until you're ready to eat.

Just before serving, sprinkle the salad with salt and pepper. Drizzle the orange juice,
add a splash of oil, and toss.

*Tip: The mango is best when it's still a little green and firm. It's easier to peel and
slice but still juicy and delicious.*

PREP TIME	COOK TIME	SERVES
15 minutes	*0 minutes*	*Family of 6*

They say imitation is the best form of flattery. I say, stealing a friends recipe and making it your own is also flattering. Thanks Sharmila - *Donna*

So simple and freakin delicious. The trick is very finely slicing the cabbage. And that sesame mayo... oh my goodness! - *Donna*

DONNA'S JAPANESE STYLE

COLESLAW

INGREDIENTS

½ bag mixed salad greens
2 cups white & red cabbage (one of each)
1 large spring onion
1 tbsp sushi vinegar
1-2 tbsp Japanese mayonnaise (Kewpie)
1 small handful coriander
Salt (to taste)

METHOD

Slice cabbages finely (thin) and place in a bowl. Add the mixed salad greens.

Finely chop coriander (about ½ cup) leaves and stalks and slice the spring onions in long diagonals. Toss all salad ingredients together.

Lightly salt, toss and sprinkle with sushi vinegar and toss again.

Add Kewpie mayo just before serving, or on the side.

Tip 1: This coleslaw is also great drizzled with our sesame mayo (see sauces and dressings section).

Tip 2: You can also add julienned red capsicum and a sprinkle of sesame seeds on top for more colour and added texture!

PREP TIME	COOK TIME	SERVES
15 minutes	*0 minutes*	*Family of 6*

DONNA'S PRAWN SALAD

INGREDIENTS

½ kg shelled Prawns (fresh or frozen*)
¼ iceberg lettuce
2 firm ripe avocados
1 telegraph cucumber
½ cup of coriander
Sushi vinegar, drizzle
Olive oil, drizzle

2-3 cloves garlic, chopped
2 tbsp butter (or coconut oil)
1 small bunch parsley
Salt, pinch

METHOD

Thinly slice the lettuce and cut the avocado into bite sized chunks. Peel the cucumber in long stripes, cut into quarters long ways, de-seed then cut into bite size pieces. Lightly sprinkle with salt, gently mix together - use your fingers. Drizzle with olive oil.

Cut the coriander roughly and sprinkle over the top. Splash with sushi vinegar, and mix again. Place a few blobs of kewpie mayo around the edges. Lightly drizzle our Japanese sesame mayo and give it a quick toss with salad utensils.

PRAWNS

Melt butter (and or coconut oil) over medium heat. Sauté the garlic until golden brown and throw in the prawns and toss until they just turn a white/pink colour. Turn off the heat.

Sprinkle with parsley, mix together and pour on top of the salad. Drizzle any butter from the pan over the top of that.

Sriracha mayo, kewpie mayo and sesame dressing all go beautifully with this.

*Tip: If you have *frozen prawns, you can quickly thaw them in a bowl of cold water. Keep rinsing until the water stops freezing, drain once thawed and splash with fish sauce. Cover and let them soak while you prepare the rest of the ingredients. Pour off the excess fish sauce just before you cook.*

PREP TIME
15 minutes

COOK TIME
5 minutes

SERVES
Family of 6

I love prawn cocktails and salad
and avocado and Japanese dressings
... so I put it all together - *Donna*

I tried this salad at a café near work and figured out the ingredients. I feel like a real smarty pants. Who knew you could eat Bok Choy raw! - *Donna*

THAI CHICKEN &
CUCUMBER SALAD

INGREDIENTS

500g Chicken, cooked and shredded
¼ cucumber (med-large size)
1 small red capsicum
½ red onion
1 small bunch Shanghai bok choy
1 small bunch coriander
3 tbsp Thai sweet chilli sauce
½ cup roasted salted peanuts

METHOD

Gently warm the peanuts in a dry pan or roast them briefly in the oven. You don't want to burn them, just roast them slightly. Roughly break/chop them into pieces and set aside.

Peel the cucumber in long stripes, deseed and chop into small pieces. In a large salad bowl add the cucumber and finely dicely small red capsicum.

Wash, and cut the bottoms off the bok choy. Slice into bite sized pieces and add to bowl. Dice the red onion (wash in cold water - this removes the burn from the onion), chop up the coriander and add to the bowl.

Mix all the vegetables together. Add sweet chillii sauce and gently toss. Add the cooked chicken and toss together throughly.

Lastly sprinkle with peanuts and serve.

Tip: We like to mix it up loosely by hand as it spreads the sauce around evenly.

PREP TIME	COOK TIME	SERVES	
10 minutes	*0 minutes*	*Family of 6*	35

ASIAN INFL

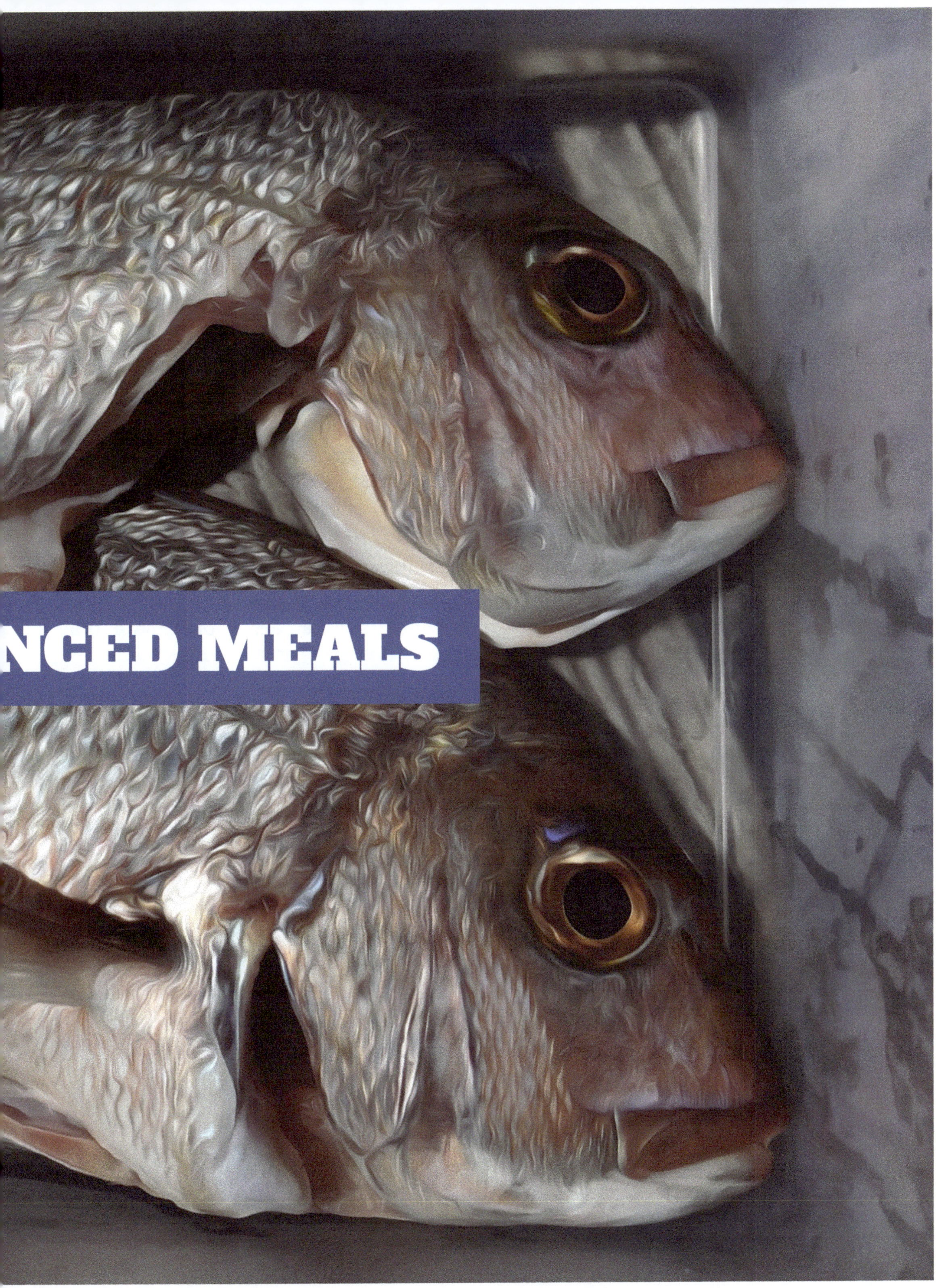

NCED MEALS

BBQ PORK

INGREDIENTS

1kg Pork belly
Ginger, 2cm - slice into little sticks
½ tsp Chinese five spice
2 tbsp rice wine
2 tbsp char siu sauce
1 tbsp hoisin sauce
1 tbsp honey
1 tbsp light soy sauce

METHOD

NB: When we cook this, we don't use measurements. We pour on the sauces until it smells, or tastes right. The measurements above are approximate, it's a fluid recipe that doesn't have to be exact. Trust your nose and personal preferences.

Combine all ingredients together (except the pork) to make a sauce and set aside in a very large bowl. Smell/taste and add more if it's not enough.

Trim the pork to remove skin. Cut into thin slices. Add the pork to the sauce and stir to coat the meat.

Marinate for at least 1 hour. It can sit in fridge overnight for extra flavour. Place the marinated pork into an oven-proof dish.

Bake at 180°C fan bake for 45 minutes to 1 hour.

Serve with steamed rice and bok choy (see first recipe).

Tip: You could marinate and cook the whole pork piece and slice up after too. You will probably have to cook it a little longer. Cutting it up before hand ensures more marinade per piece especially if you leave it over night and the flavour spreads right through.

PREP TIME	COOK TIME	SERVES
1 hr 20 minutes	45 - 60 minutes	Family of 6

Don't let Jordan near this once its cooked - he'll eat it all! - *Max*

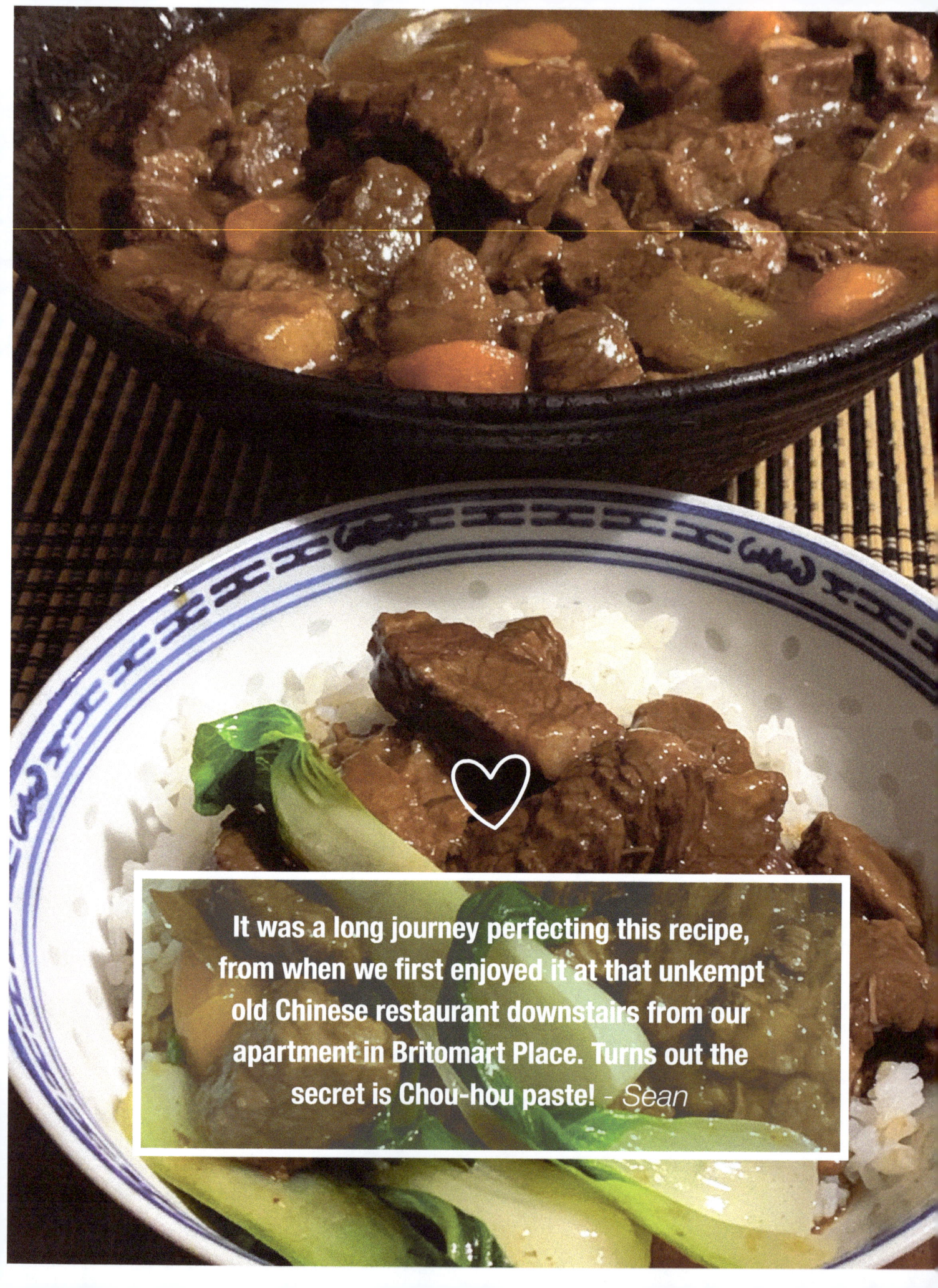

It was a long journey perfecting this recipe, from when we first enjoyed it at that unkempt old Chinese restaurant downstairs from our apartment in Britomart Place. Turns out the secret is Chou-hou paste! - *Sean*

CANTONESE STYLE

BRAISED BRISKET

INGREDIENTS

1kg Brisket, boneless *or* 2kg brisket bone
2 carrots
2 sticks celery
2 tbsp light soy sauce
1 tbsp dark soy sauce
2 tbsp chou hou paste
2 bay leaves
6 star anise
1 tbsp coconut oil
1 tsp Chinese five spice
½ cup Chinese rice wine
2 tsp sugar
1 tbsp coconut oil
Water to cover

THICKENING PASTE

3 tbsp cornflour
1 tbsp water
(add more water, a little at a time to be sure to get a slow running paste)

METHOD

Cut brisket into small chunks.

Add coconut oil to a large heavy pot/casserole dish and lightly brown the meat. Chop the carrots and celery chunky and add the chopped vegetables to the dish and fry, until a little golden brown.

Add soy sauces, paste, spices, stir and cover with water.

Braise for at least 2 ½ hours - the longer the better. In the last 10 minutes you can add some more celery and carrots for colour and texture. Thicken with the thickening paste.

Serve with rice and bok choy.

Tip: If you leave it overnight, then reheat it, it will melt in your mouth.

PREP TIME	COOK TIME	SERVES
10-15 minutes	*2 ½ hours*	*Family of 6*

CANTONESE STEAMED FISH

INGREDIENTS

1 fresh whole white fish, *or* whole flounder/sole
2 spring onions
½ bunch coriander
Ginger, 4cm
¼ cup rice wine
Salt, to taste
Sesame oil, drizzle

METHOD

Use a fresh, gutted and descaled whole fish. Make about 5-6 diagonal cuts over each side of the fish.

Place the fish in the center of a big piece of foil (enough to cover completely but a little loose so there's room to steam).

Chop the spring onions and fresh coriander loosely. Finely slice the ginger and cut into match sticks. Surround and cover the fish with the spring onions, coriander and ginger. Sprinkle with salt, drizzle with sesame oil and pour rice wine over it.

Cover with foil.

Fan bake in the oven at 150°C for approximately 15-20 minutes. You don't want it to be breaking apart too much, but soft and flakey is cooked. Take it out of the oven and leave covered until you're just about ready to serve.

Tip: Firm white fish fillets Snapper, Gurnard or Terakihi are best. Flounder was my Mum and Dad's favourite when we were growing up.

PREP TIME	COOK TIME	SERVES
15 minutes	*20 minutes*	*Family of 6 (or just Grandpop)*

There must be a chinese name for this, but I can't for the life of me remember what it is - *Sean*

Alia goes nuts for this one!
I'm sooo pleased with myself that
I hailed it first attempt.
A favourite from our
Singapore days - *Sean*

CHAR KWAY TEOW

HAWKER STYLE NOODLES

INGREDIENTS

250g Prawns 1/2 cup fresh Cockles
200g Pork, 2 Lup Cheong (chinese sausage)
1kg rice noodles, fresh
1 small bag bean spouts
1 tsp belacan (dried shrimp paste)
3 tbsp coconut or rice bran oil
¼ bunch garlic chives
2-3 cloves garlic
2 tbsp light soy sauce
1 tbsp dark soy sauce
2 tbsp Kecap manis sauce
Sriracha (medium or hot), to taste

* OMELETTE

2 eggs
1 tbsp butter

Melt a knob of butter in a frying pan. Crack 2 eggs into a bowl briefly whisk and pour into a hot pan. Swirl to spread across the whole pan so its very thin. It should be cooked in less than a minute, flip it (if you can) then slide it out of the pan onto a plate and put aside.

METHOD

Precook the pork (fry, steam or roast). Slice the Lup Cheong into thin ovals. Make a thin plain egg **omelette***, roll it up and slice into small pieces.

Chop chives into 3cm lengths, crush garlic and finely dice.

In a wok, heat coconut or rice bran oil. Stir fry garlic, lup cheong, prawns (or chicken), add garlic chives, turn off the heat and put aside in a separate bowl.

Stir fry the noodles with sauces and belacan, then add in the other ingredients. Add cockles now. Loosley combine and add a couple of handfuls of bean sprouts. Toss again and serve.

Tip: The secret is lots of kecap manis. If you have a super hot wok, you can cook it hawker style. We have never had to use belacan before, but now it's in our fridge all the time. It smells pretty pungent so keep it in a sealed container or bag after you've opened it.

PREP TIME	COOK TIME	SERVES
20 minutes	35 minutes	Family of 6

SWEET CHILLI

CHICKEN WINGS

INGREDIENTS

2 kg Chicken wings
6 cloves garlic
2 tbsp light soy sauce
2 tbsp dark soy sauce
2 tbsp sweet chilli sauce

3 caps Chinese rice wine
1 tsp sriracha or chilli oil
2 tbsp sesame oil
1 tbsp plain cooking oil (not olive)

METHOD

NB: Add the amount of sauces you prefer. Donna likes to use more of the dark soy and sweet chilli sauce and Sean prefers to use less of the dark soy and chilli and more of the light soy. Both options are great.

Clean the chicken wings with boiling water and dry with paper towels (this tightens the chicken skin and helps to make it crispy). Separate winglet from drumlet if they're whole.

Crush and finely chop garlic, pop into a bowl with the chicken pieces. Add a splash of chinese rice wine, a small drizzle of sesame oil and sriracha sauce. Pour light and dark soy and sweet chilli sauce over the chicken and cover it generously. Mix everything in a big bowl until it smells right. Marinate for as long as you have - minimum 15 minutes.

Arrange in a single layer in a roasting pan.

Bake at 160°C for 40-45 minutes, turning a couple of times so they brown evenly.

Tip: Just before dishing up, drizzle with sweet chilli sauce and a sprinkling of sesame seeds.

PREP TIME
10 minutes

COOK TIME
40-45 minutes

SERVES
Family of 6

This is one of our regular meals,
it's something everyone likes
and is easy to make - *Donna*

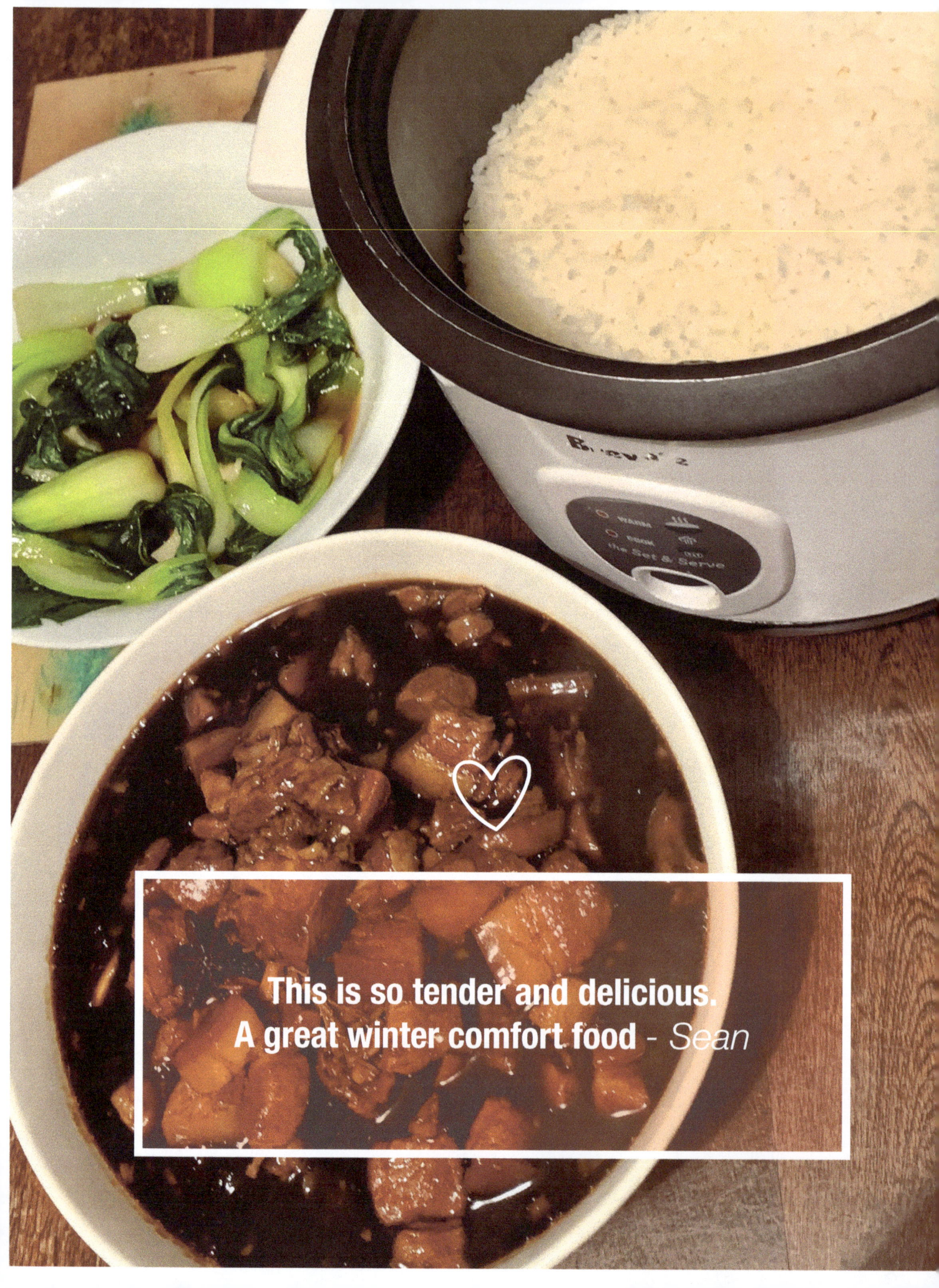

This is so tender and delicious.
A great winter comfort food - *Sean*

CHINESE RED PORK

INGREDIENTS

1kg Pork slices (pork belly)
4 tbsp raw sugar
¾ cup light soy sauce
2 tbsp dark soy sauce
5cm ginger bruised (smash it)
3 cups rice wine
4 star anise

THICKENING PASTE

3 tbsp cornflour
1 tbsp water
(add more water a little at a time
to get a slow running paste)

METHOD

Put the pork in a pot, cover with cold water and boil for 5 minutes. Wash and strain the pork well under cold water.

Add cleaned pork, rice wine, ginger and star anise to a large pot. Add enough water to cover the pork. Bring to the boil, then simmer for 40 minutes.

Add soy sauce, plus the sugar, stir and simmer for a further 20 minutes. The liquid should reduce by a third. The more you reduce it the redder it will become.

You can thicken it with a little thickening paste.

Serve with steamed rice and bok choy.

Tip: You may want to add a little food colouring to it to make it redder, if you do decide to do this put it in just as you start to simmer - it'll look pink but that's fine because as it reduces it will get darker.

PREP TIME	COOK TIME	SERVES
20 minutes	1 hr	Family of 6

HAINANESE CHICKEN RICE

INGREDIENTS

1 free-range (preferred) whole Chicken
1 chicken frame and 2 drum sticks (for stock)
2 carrots
2 sticks celery
Ginger, 6cm
2 spring onions
2-3 pandan leaves
2 tbsp light soy

METHOD

NB: Poached chicken can look under-cooked and sometimes it can be a little pink around the bone. You will know it's cooked when the juices run clear (not pink), making it juicy, tasty and delicious.

Take whole chicken and pour boiling water over it. Exfoliate the skin by rubbing it all over with salt. Rinse and pat dry.

Make a quick stock by ¾ filling stock pot with boiled water. Use chicken frames/thighs/drums, carrot quartered long ways, celery cut in half, smash and split the ginger into 3 bits and add pandan and soy last. If you don't have time or ingredients to make a stock, a tetrapak ready made stock is a great alternative option.

Bring your stock to boil. Turn off and add the whole chicken ensuring it is covered with water (if there's not enough room in the pot, remove the frames). Add a little more boiling water if you have to, or put something on top of the chicken to stop it floating. Leave the lid on.

Poach the chicken for 2-3 hours. If the chicken is big, remove half way through, reheat the stock, turn off and replace the chicken into the pot. NEVER boil the chicken.

Set aside the chicken to drain and cool a bit before chopping into chunks and serve with rice and choy. Good with keyung yook, nuoc cham and a hot sauce on the side.

PREP TIME	COOK TIME	SERVES
10 minutes	*2-3 hours*	*Family of 6*

My Malaysian friend was quite impressed that I'd figured out the ingredients to poach the chicken, especially the pandan leaf. I feel quite chuffed about that - *Donna*

This is basically candied chicken.
No wonder it's
a family favourite. - *Donna*

TERIYAKI CHICKEN

INGREDIENTS

750g Chicken boneless thigh fillets
3 tbsp cornflour
3 tbsp soy sauce
3 tbsp sake
2 tbsp mirin
3 tbsp raw or brown sugar
Rice bran oil, or coconut oil to cook

METHOD

Chop the chicken thighs into bite-sized pieces.

Coat the chicken in cornflour.

Fry until golden brown, shaking the pan gently and using a paper towel to soak up any excess fat.

Mix all the other ingredients together in a bowl then pour over the chicken. Reduce the heat to low and cook until the sauce thickens.

Sometimes it can be too thick - add a splash or two of water to stop it going gluggy and lumpy.

Serve with steamed rice and sliced cucumber.

Tip: If the sauce thickens too quickly or is very thick, don't be afraid to add a little water to the pan, a tablespoon at time until you reach the right consistency.

PREP TIME
10 minutes

COOK TIME
35 minutes

SERVES
Family of 6

MĀMĀ'S SIU GAI

CHINESE ROAST CHICKEN

INGREDIENTS
1 free-range or organic Chicken
2-3 cloves garlic
2 spring onion sticks (not whole)
Ginger, 4 cm
3 caps rice wine
1 tsp Chinese five spice
1 tbsp honey (any type works)

METHOD
NB: We're not sure of the measurement of the rice wine. We just splash a bit on, enough on to wet it so the spices stick to the skin.

Pour boiling water over chicken (this helps tighten the skin). Pat dry. Pour rice wine over the chicken and sprinkle with salt and five spice. Rub all over to spread evenly around the chicken

Stuff the chicken interior with crushed garlic, thick sliced ginger and the spring onion cut into pieces to fit inside the chicken.

Fan bake at 180°C for approximately 45 minutes.

Remove the stuffing from the chicken interior and put aside. Chop chicken and place in a serving dish.

To make the gravy, add honey to the roasting juices, heat and stir until dissolved.

Pour gravy over the chicken, or serve it separately.

PREP TIME
20 minutes

COOK TIME
45 minutes

SERVES
Family of 6

Siu means roasted She-yao
is Soy. I found this very confusing
at first because they sound so similar.
Now I know better *- Donna*

A wonderful family tradition.
Reminds us of Māmā every time we
cook it. Especially in our 4th generation
careen casserole dish! - *Sean*

MĀMĀ'S SHE-YAO GAI

SOY CHICKEN

INGREDIENTS

1 free-range (preferred) whole Chicken
2 garlic cloves
3-4 tbsp light soy sauce
¼ cup water
2 tsp Chinese five spice
2 tbsp raw sugar
4 caps rice wine* (optional)

THICKENING PASTE

3 tbsp cornflour
1 tbsp water
(add more water a little at a time to get a slow running paste)

METHOD

Put oil into your casserole dish and heat. Squash a couple of garlic cloves to flavour the oil. When garlic is lightly browned, remove and throw away. Place the chicken into the dish and brown each side.

Add sauces, water, (*rice wine), five spice and raw sugar and put the lid on to cover chicken.

Turn down the heat and simmer for about 30-40 minutes or until tender. Turn once or twice to ensure the chicken is evenly coated and cooked.

Remove chicken, cut into pieces and place in a serving dish.

Add thickening paste to jup**. Once it has a nice syrupy consistency pour over the chicken.

Serve with steamed vegetables and rice.

Tip: Make sure you have a strong fork and tongs to lift and turn the chicken when you're browning it.

** *Jup is the juices created when cooking this dish.*

PREP TIME	COOK TIME	SERVES
15 minutes	*45 minutes*	*Family of 6*

SWEET 'N' SOUR PORK

INGREDIENTS

1kg Pork slices *or* pork belly slices
Ginger, 4cm
2 tbsp rice wine
2 tbsp soy sauce
2-3 garlic, crushed
1 large onion
2 carrots
2 sticks celery
½ red capsicum
1 courgette

SWEET 'N' SOUR SAUCE

½ cup tomato sauce
2 tbsp sugar
¼ cup vinegar
2 tbsp water

THICKENING PASTE

1 tbsp cornflour
1 tsp water
*(add more water a little at a time
to get a slow running paste)*

METHOD

Slice the pork into bite-sized pieces. In a separate bowl add finely diced ginger, rice wine and soy sauce. Mix well. Add your pork, cover and stand aside.

Chop all the vegetables into similar sized pieces (so they cook evenly). Take a wok or fry pan, add oil and heat. When the pan starts to smoke add the garlic and vegetables and quickly stir fry. Cook no longer than 2 minutes. Once cooked, but still crunchy, set aside in a bowl.

In a small saucepan combine your sweet 'n' sour sauce ingredients. Simmer for 5 minutes, then stir in the thickening past. Set aside and keep it warm.

Stir fry the marinated pork. When the pork is just cooked through, add the cooked vegetables and sauce to the wok. Combine quickly. Remove from heat and take the wok or fry pan directly to the table and serve onto the rice.

Tip 1: When making the sauce, try make it a little tangier that you like. Once it's added to the dish it becomes more savoury because of the other juices.

Tip 2: You could add pineapple, fresh or canned and a handful of bean sprouts sprinkled on top. This also adds a nice fresh crunch.

PREP TIME
15 minutes

COOK TIME
15 minutes

SERVES
Family of 6 (or just Jordan)

Jordan can demolish this entire dish all by himself. Something to keep in mind when serving - *Donna*

NANA JACQUI'S FAVOURITE -

INGREDIENTS
1-2 whole Fish (gutted, cleaned, dried)
2-3 tbsp cornflour
2-3 cups any flavourless oil
2 tbsp fish sauce
1 tbsp lime juice
1/3 cup water
1 tsp sweet chilli sauce
½ tbsp tamarind paste
1 tbsp sugar - brown *or* palm
3 cloves garlic
½ cup spring onions
1 cup coriander

THICKENING PASTE
2 tbsp cornflour
1 tsp water

(add more water a little at a time until you get a slow running paste)

METHOD
Wash and pat dry the fish and make about 4-5 diagonal slash/slices on each side of the fish, approximately 1 inch apart. Season with fish sauce. Smooth/rub over both sides of the fish with cornflour.

Chop spring onions and ½ a cup of fresh coriander. Put aside.

In a saucepan combine all the liquid ingredients along with finely chopped garlic, sugar and remaining ½ cup chopped coriander (include stems and root) and a splash of sriracha or sweet chili sauce.

Simmer and adjust flavour until it tastes Thai = sweet, sour, salty, hot. Reduce a little, add thickening paste, turn off and keep aside.

Cook the fish now. See next page.

Tip 1: We love to use fresh Snapper, because it's a local fish, usually caught by Grandpop. You can use any white fleshed fish - it will taste amazing.

Tip 2: Have all your cooking tools ready beforehand. Ideally keep all pets and little kids out of the kitchen. Hot oil needs to be handled carefully!

PREP TIME
20 minutes

COOK TIME
10-15 minutes

SERVES
Family of 6

THAI DEEP FRIED FISH

COOKING THE FISH

Heat the oil in a separate fry pan deep enough to take a whole fish. To check if the oil is ready, dip a wooden chopstick into it. If it sizzles, the oil is ready.

Firmly but gently lower the fish into the oil sliding it gently away from you. It should bubble up and make a wonderful sound almost like a water fall. Try and get the tail fried as well. Spoon the hot oil over the top of the fish, when the fins start to brown, gently turn it over, hold a spatular over the meaty bit so none of it falls off. Leave on that side briefly, about 20-30 seconds just to finish it off.

Turn off the pan and remove fish to a large serving dish. Sprinkle generously with spring onion and coriander, pour over still hot sauce and sprinkle a few more herbs on top.

Nana Jacqui's Cooks Beach favourite! We're so spoiled, with Grandpop catching fresh snapper for us daily. This one Sean figured out by himself too - *Donna*

This is so addictive!
Best smelling
marinade EVER - *Donna*

FRIED PORK

INGREDIENTS

1kg Pork
3 tbsp shallots *or* red onion
3-4 cloves garlic
2 tbsp cooking oil *(coconut is preferred, but any cooking oil is fine)*

MARINADE

¼ cup raw or palm sugar
1 tbsp fish sauce
½ tbsp Kecap manis sauce
½ tbsp black pepper
3 tbsp cooking oil (not olive)

FIXINGS

2-3 spring onions
Fresh mint
Fresh coriander
Fresh Thai basil
1 small bag bean sprouts

METHOD

Slice the pork into bite-sized pieces and combine with the marinade for a minimum of 15 minutes.

In a fry pan heat the oil and cook the pork in small batches until crispy and still moist.

While that is marinating, roughly chop all herbs (fixings). The idea is that once the pork is cooked you add these to the dish at your own discretion. Sprinkle a small handful of herbs on top of the meat for extra flavour and texture.

Serve with rich and the Vietnamese fixings. So easy, so yummy!

Tip: Nuoc cham goes great with this as well. We've been known to eat the pork and nothing else for dinner.

PREP TIME	COOK TIME	SERVES
15 minutes	*15 minutes*	*Family of 6*

BEEF BULGOGI

MEAT INGREDIENTS

1kg Rump Steak
3 tbsp soya sauce
3 tbsp water
2 tsp sugar
Ground black pepper
2 cloves garlic, diced
1 tbsp grated ginger
1 whole spring onion, finely chopped
2 tbsp roasted ground sesame seeds

SAUCE INGREDIENTS

Splash chilli sauce
1 tsp bean paste
3 tbsp soya sauce
2 tbsp sesame seeds
2 tbsp rice wine
2 cloves crushed garlic
1 tbsp grated ginger
2 tbsp spring onions
2 tsp sugar - raw or brown
2 tbsp water

METHOD

Slice the rump thinly and put into a deep bowl. Add all the meat ingredients and marinate for a minimum ½ hour.

Make the sauce in a bowl and set aside.

Hot wok the meat in small batches (to fry not broil), serve straight away onto rice with a little of the sauce drizzled over the top.

Tip: Leave to marinate overnight to make it melt in your mouth.

PREP TIME
45 minutes

COOK TIME
15 minutes

SERVES
Family of 6

When I make this, I grind the
sesame seeds to a paste.
Donna is too lazy to do that.
I think my way is better - *Sean*

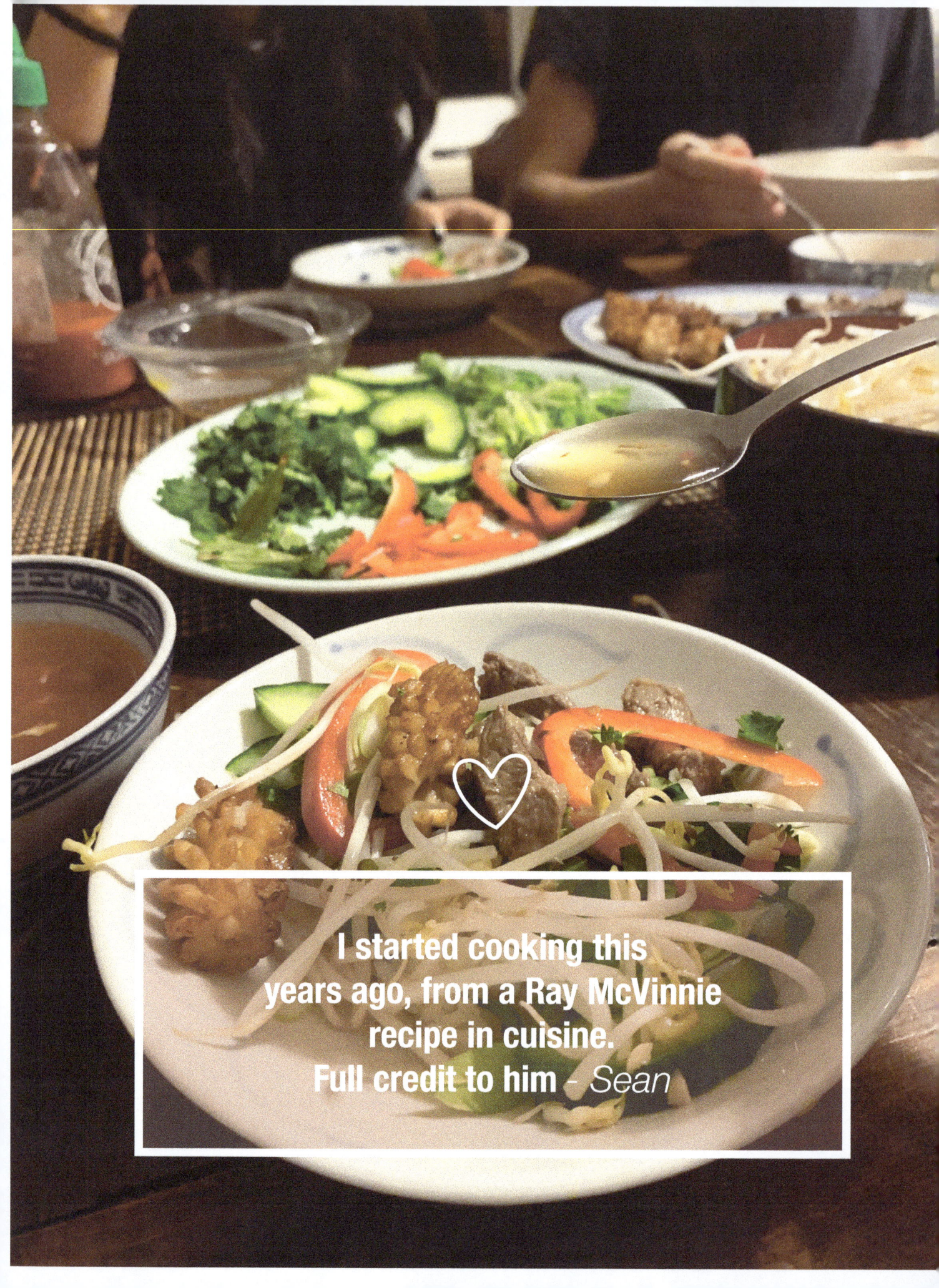

I started cooking this
years ago, from a Ray McVinnie
recipe in cuisine.
Full credit to him - *Sean*

VIETNAMESE BBQ

INGREDIENTS

500g Rump steak
500g Chicken
500g Squid sheets (not tubes)
¼ cup coriander
2 tbsp Thai basil
2 tbsp Vietnamese mint

MARINADE

¼ cup palm *or* brown sugar
4 cloves garlic
1 tsp grated fresh ginger
2 tbsp light soy sauce
¼ cup fish sauce
2 tbsp lime juice

METHOD

Slice all protein into thin bite-sized pieces.

Score the squid in a crosshatch pattern, approximately 1cm apart. Cut into little rectangle sizes.

Mix all ingredients (except fresh herbs) in a decent sized bowl. Marinate all the protein together (except chicken, marinate in a separate bowl) for approximately 30 minutes.

Chop all fresh herbs, combine and set aside.

Spark up the BBQ. If you don't have a BBQ, you could use a hot plate, robata grill or fry pan.

Cook quickly (1-2 minutes) and serve immediately accompanied by steamed rice. Sprinkle some fresh herbs on top if preferred.

Tip 1: Have all your serving dishes ready beforehand.

Tip 2: Serve with Nuoc Cham (see the recipe in our mayo's and sauces section) and sweet chilli sauce.

Tip 3: Great served with salads or grilled vegetables, eg, courgette, capsicums, beans or eggplant.

PREP TIME	COOK TIME	SERVES
35 minutes	*10 minutes*	*Family of 6*

WESTER

TYLE FOOD

FLUFFY SCRAMBLED EGGS

INGREDIENTS

2 eggs
1 pinch of Salt
Pepper to season
2 tsp fresh water
1 tbsp butter

METHOD

Whisk the eggs, salt, pepper and water together.

Put a decent sized tablespoon of butter in a medium-hot pan, once melted add the egg mixture. Stir and gently move the egg around with a spatular or spoon. Once it's nearly cooked (less than a minute cooking) take off the heat. They'll finish cooking as you serve them onto your plate.

You can use olive oil, but butter is better (especially NZ butter from grass fed, outdoor cows).

Tip 1: If you are cooking for more people, add 2 eggs per person

Tip 2: Why add water to the eggs? The water in the egg turns to steam as it cooks. As the water evaporates it creates air/bubbles in the eggs, making them fluffier and lighter than if you were to use cream or milk.

PREP TIME	COOK TIME	SERVES
1 minute	*2 minutes*	*1 adult*

We add a little water.
"The Mentalist" TV show
taught us this - *Sean*

Sean's most excellent burger!
Premium ingredients and
unfussy cooking brings it
together perfectly - *Donna*

THE ORIGINAL SLACKBURGER

INGREDIENTS

500g Beef mince
6 brioche buns
Dijonnaise
12 cheese slices (edam or swiss)
Kewpie mayonnaise

Lettuce
Sliced gherkins
Tomato sauce
Caramalised red onions
Salt & pepper

METHOD

Cut buns in half, put a swirl of dijonnaise on both sides, place a slice of cheese on both and melt under the grill.

While that is grilling, form the mince into patties and fry. Do not season the mince patties while grilling them.

Add a swirl of mayo to the top side of the buns and a generous swirl of tomato sauce to the bottoms. Add the hot pattie, season with salt and pepper and another swirl of tomato sauce. Then add a dollop of caramelised onion on top of that. Add lettuce and gherkin to the top bun, slap them together and there's your Original Slackburger.

Tip: Feel free to add tomatoes, fried eggs or whatever extras you like.

THE SLACK FAMILY OF BURGERS

• **The Don Burger** - original with tomato relish, sliced beetroot and a fried egg

• **KimCheese Burger** - swap lettuce for Kimchi

• **The Ninjalia** - teriyaki chicken with mum's sesame mayo

• **Tate Burger** - has a couple of slices of beetroot and a heap of gherkin slices

• **Big Max Burger** - swap out the mince for a small piece of steak

PREP TIME	COOK TIME	SERVES	
15 minutes	*20 minutes*	6	

BACON PESTO PASTA

INGREDIENTS

250g Speck *or* Pancetta (or regular bacon)
1 packet penne or spaghetti
25g butter
1 tbsp olive oil
4-5 tbsp basil pesto (store bought, or freshly made)
1 litre water

METHOD

Boil the pasta in a large pot of water, for as long as specified on the packet. Add a few pinches of salt. When the pasta is cooked through (test it), drain and set aside.

In a fry pan, add olive oil and fry the speck/pancetta/bacon until nice and crispy. Remove from pan and chop into small bits. Save the pan with the bacon fat still in it and put aside. Put bacon bits into a separate bowl and also set aside.

Take the cooked pasta and place into the pan with the bacon fat. Tongs are good to stir it around and fold the fat through. Once it's well coated, add and stir in the pesto then lastly the bacon pieces.

Mix well, then serve.

Tip 1: Try and get good quality ingredients for bacon, pesto and pasta.

Tip 2: For added flavour - sprinkle on top a little grated parmesan cheese and a small handful of chopped fresh parsley.

PREP TIME
10 minutes

COOK TIME
15 minutes

SERVES
Family of 6

The simplest recipe and
one of our family faves - *Sean*

Sean's absolute
all time favourite! - *Donna*

MUM'S OXTAIL STEW

INGREDIENTS

2kg Oxtail
½ head celery
2 carrots
1 tbsp mild curry powder
2 tbsp light soy sauce
1 tbsp dark soy sauce
2 cloves garlic
3 bay leaves
¼ cup Chinese rice wine

THICKENING PASTE

3 tbsp cornflour
1 tbsp water
(add more water a little at a time to get a slow running paste)

METHOD

Fry the oxtail in a casserole dish (or big heavy pot) until brown on all sides.

Chop the vegetables chunky and add to the pot. Cover with water.

Add remaining ingredients and simmer for at least 2 hours.

Approximately 10 minutes before cooking time is up, add some more chopped celery so you get a bit of crunch and colour.

Thicken, then serve in big bowls with rice.

Tip: The longer you simmer it, the more tender it becomes.

PREP TIME
15 minutes

COOK TIME
2-3 hours

SERVES
Family of 6

AMERICAN BBQ SPARE RIBS

INGREDIENTS

1-2 kg Pork spare ribs
¼ cups water
1 ½ cups cider vinegar
¾ cup brown sugar (pack firmly)
2 tbsp tomato paste
2 cups tomato sauce
4 cloves crushed garlic
1 tsp sriracha

SPICE RUB

2 tbsp paprika
2 tbsp mustard powder
1 tbsp salt
2 tsp allspice
½ tbsp cumin
½ tbsp ground coriander
Ground pepper chilli

METHOD

Wash and dry the pork ribs.

Mix the dry ingredients for the spice rub together in a bowl. Once mixed rub it all over the pork ribs. Cover tightly with foil and bake in a low oven (125°C) for 1 hour per kg. Remove and pour some of the baking juice off into a separate container.

Mix all of the other ingredients into a bowl and add a little more mustard powder and paprika. Let that stand for a while to infuse. Add some of the baking juices to the sauce if you like.

Heat BBQ to high, then turn to low. Mix half of the BBQ sauce with the reserved baking juices and coat the ribs. Cook for half hour, basting and turning every five minutes.

Tip: This is a great recipe to involve the kids in. Get them used to handling hot stuff and being attentive. For the grown ups, a cold beer or rum and a good debate make the ribs enjoyable even before you've eaten them.

PREP TIME
20 minutes

COOK TIME
2 hours approx

SERVES
Family of 6 (or one teenage boy)

Part two of my adventures in barbecuing.
Makes me want to try BBQ brisket.
Mmmm yum! - *Sean*

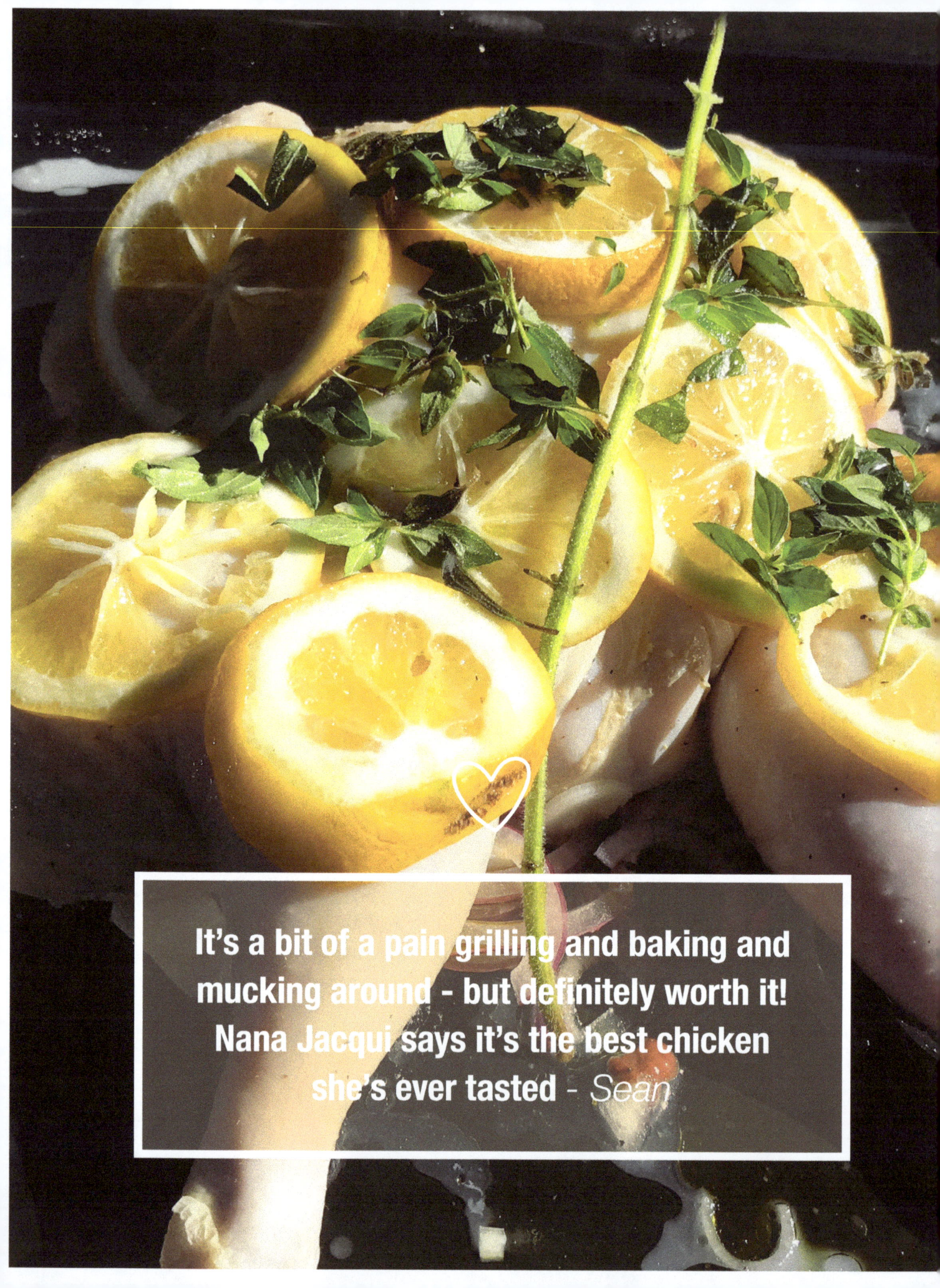

It's a bit of a pain grilling and baking and mucking around - but definitely worth it! Nana Jacqui says it's the best chicken she's ever tasted - *Sean*

ROAST CHICKEN

INGREDIENTS

1 free-range whole Chicken
Pinch sea salt
Fresh ground black pepper
1 onion, finely sliced
2 lemons
1 tbsp fresh oregano, finely chopped
5 tbsp olive oil

METHOD

Butterfly chicken along the backbone. If you have kitchen scissors, use them, it's much easier. Flatten the chicken once butterflied, season both sides with salt and pepper. Spread your onion slices over the bottom of a large baking dish and lay the chicken on top.

Rub 2 tbsp of olive oil onto the surface of chicken and sprinkle with oregano. Cut one lemon into even slices and lay them flat all over the top of the chicken. Marinate for one hour (minimum).

Remove the lemon slices from the chicken and place the chicken back on the baking tray. Brown both sides under a hot grill to crisp up the skin then put the chicken back in the oven and roast at 250°C for 15 minutes.

Baste the chicken with more olive oil and lemon juice. Roast for approximately 40 minutes until fully cooked. Serve with the garlic yoghurt, tomato relish and other Middle Eastern type dressings.

Tip: This is one of three recipes in this book that isn't "quick and easy". Make sure you have the time to do it, to get it just right. It's definitely worth giving it a go and well worth the wait.

PREP TIME
30 minutes

COOK TIME
1 hour

SERVES
Family of 6, or 2 very hungry

TATE'S ROASPIE CHICKEN

INGREDIENTS

Whole free-range or organic Chicken
Fresh herbs - thyme, sage, oregano, what ever you have
6+ garlic cloves
2-3 tbsp of olive oil (to rub)
½ lemon
Salt

METHOD

Firstly, wash the chicken in cold water, then pour boiling water over it to refresh and tighten the skin. Rub with salt to exfoliate and pat dry.

Split the chicken down the spine and lay flat in the baking tray.

Slip the garlic and herbs under the skin at the breast and thighs.

Put lemon juice and olive oil in your hand, then rub/massage all over the chicken. Sprinkle the chicken all over with a fine layer of salt.

Fan bake for 45 minutes at 175°C.

Use the left over chicken juice in the roasting dish to make a gravy.

Tip: Cleaning and drying the chicken makes the skin crisp and papery.

PREP TIME
10 minutes

COOK TIME
45 minutes

SERVES
Family of 6

I love that Tate made up
her own words for things
when she was little - *Donna*

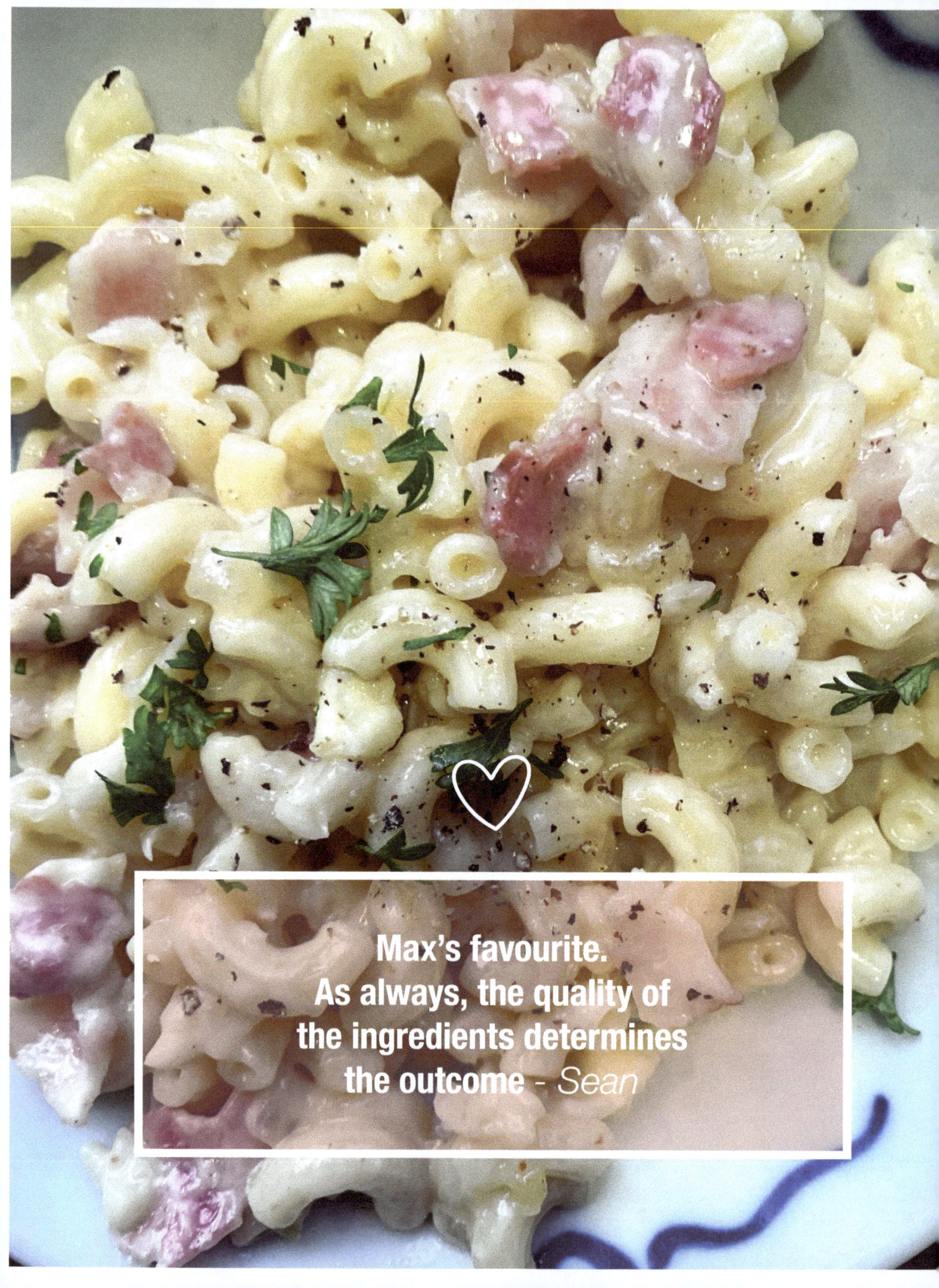

Max's favourite.
As always, the quality of
the ingredients determines
the outcome - *Sean*

SEAN'S MACARONI CHEESE

INGREDIENTS

250g Bacon, Pancetta *or* Speck
1 ½ finely chopped onions
½ cauliflower
500g macaroni
50g butter
2 tbsp flour

2 tsp mustard powder
1 tsp ground black pepper
250g edam cheese
40g parmesan cheese
300ml organic full cream milk
Olive oil for frying

METHOD

Boil the pasta in plenty of salted water for the duration stated on the packet. Drain and set aside.

Dice the onions and cut the bacon into small pieces. Break the cauliflower into tiny florets (like rice) and steep in the pasta water. Drain. Fry the bacon in plenty of olive oil.

Remove the bacon, but keep the oil in the pan and fry the onions until translucent. Toss the cauliflower and bacon back in the pan and set aside.

In the pasta pot melt the butter over a low heat. Mix the flour, mustard, salt and pepper in a small bowl then tip into the pot.

Whisk for a couple of minutes over the low heat until the flour is cooked. This is the most important step. Slowly add the milk, whisking constantly. Once you have a good, thick consistency for the white sauce turn it off and add the grated cheeses. Mix until combined.

Toss the macaroni in the pan with the bacon and onion then pour it all back into the pot with the cheese sauce. Stir.

Other people then bake the macaroni cheese to give it a crust, but those people are weird.

PREP TIME	COOK TIME	SERVES
20 minutes	*20 minutes*	*Family of 6*

SALMON HASH

INGREDIENTS

6 potatoes, chopped and boiled (Agria is best)
1 onion, finely diced
1 big pinch of sugar
Butter & olive oil to fry
Salmon, smoked *or* fresh
2 tbsp chopped Italian parsley
Spring onion or fresh dill to garnish
Hollandaise, mayonnaise, or aoili

METHOD

Don't peel the potatoes! Chop them into cubes and boil for approximately 15 minutes so they're still a little firm. Drain and scuff them up in a colander and let them cool.

Fry onion in a heavy pan with oil and butter, sprinkle with a big pinch of sugar. When slightly caramelised add more butter and oil, then add and fry the potatoes.

If the salmon is raw, flash fry that until you can flake it. Put aside.

Once the potatoes have crispy bits turn off the pan, then add tuna and parsley. Roughly mix together.

Assemble the dish and drizzle with hollandaise sauce then garnish.

Tip 1: Did you know that if you put oil in the pan then the butter, it stops the butter burning? You can get more delicious buttery flavours with everything.

Tip 2: If you're doing something like pancakes, definitely use coconut oil.

PREP TIME
20 minutes

COOK TIME
10 minutes

SERVES
Family of 6

Why oh why did they ever take this
off their menu. Reminds us of
living in the Britomart Apartment,
Auckland Central - *Sean*

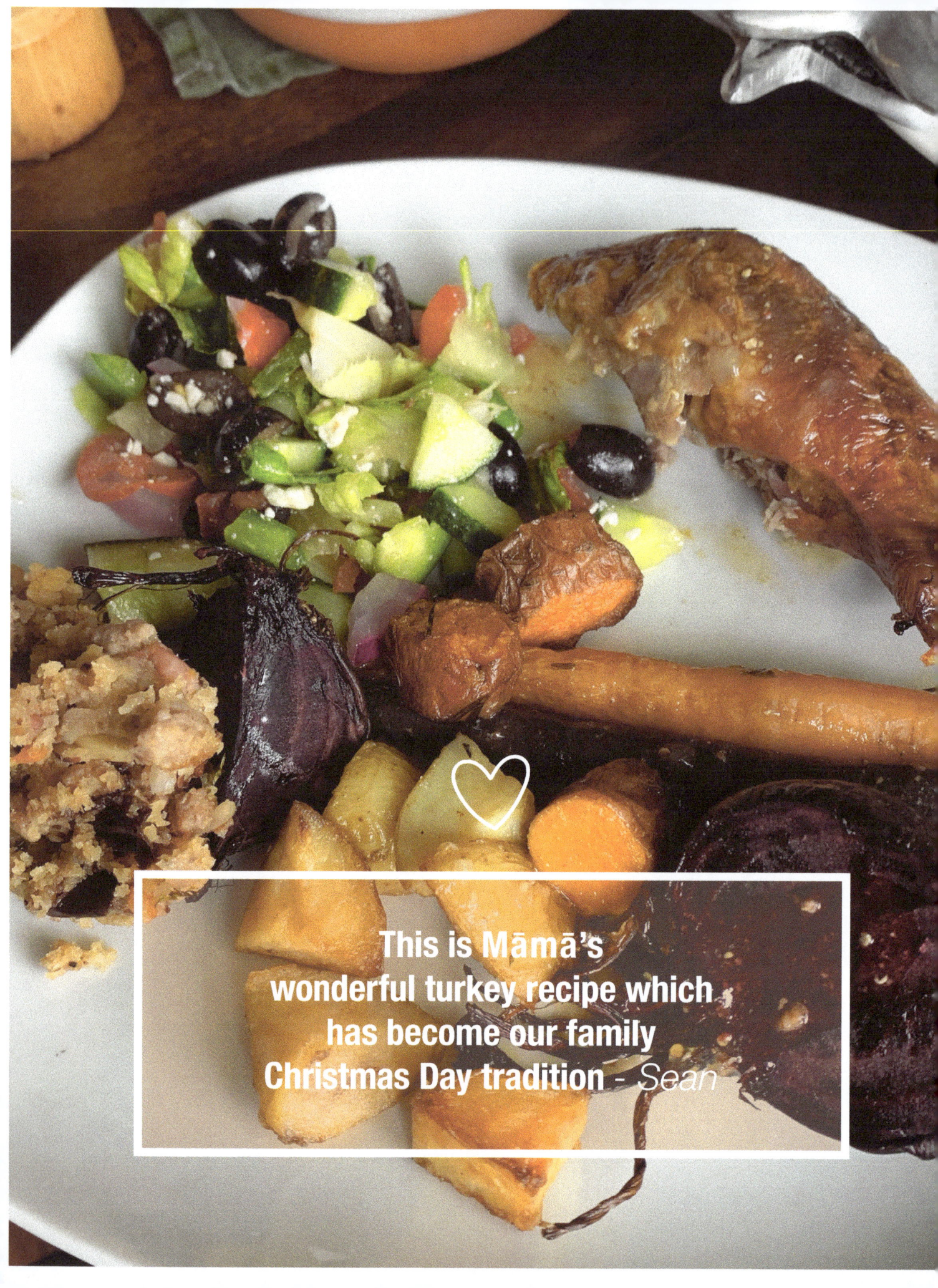

This is Māmā's
wonderful turkey recipe which
has become our family
Christmas Day tradition - *Sean*

MUM'S XMAS TURKEY

INGREDIENTS

250g onion, finely diced
150g carrots, diced
3 tbsp olive oil
250g pork mince
180g diced bacon or lardons
½ tsp cinnamon
1 cup sherry
½ cup sultanas
1 cup pitted prunes

½ cup dried apricots
1 cup chicken stock
1 cup of cooked kumara (sweet potato)
250 g breadcrumbs
½ cup italian flat-leaf parsley, diced
2 tbsp chopped oregano
4 sprigs fresh thyme
80g almonds, slivered
Salt & pepper

METHOD

For the chicken stuffing, fry off and lightly sweat the onion and carrots in a pan with olive oil. Add pork mince and bacon and turn to a high heat. Season lightly, add the cinnamon and ½ cup of sherry. Reduce on medium heat until the liquid has almost gone. Put in the dried fruits and stir well, add a little chicken stock to moisten.

Take off the heat and mix in the chopped kumara, breadcrumbs, herbs and almonds. Season to taste and moisten with chicken stock if it's too dry.
Scold the bird with boiling water to clean and refresh, then pat dry. Stuff the bird generously, but not too densely with stuffing. Secure the chicken cavity with a wooden skewer, then season the bird with salt and rub with olive oil. Surround bird in roasting dish with remaining stock and sherry. Bake at 160°C for 3 hours. Baste occasionally.

Once brown, cover with foil, whilst still allowing gaps for steam to escape. It's ready to be carved and shared.

Tip 1: This is the 2nd recipe that's a little complicated and takes a while to prepare. Luckily we do this only once a year so have alot of time to go hunting and gathering.

Tip 2: You can wrap any extra stuffing in foil or put it in a loaf tin, cover and cook at the same time as the turkey, just not for 3 hours!

PREP TIME	COOK TIME	SERVES
1 hour	*3 hours*	*Family of 8*

XMAS LEFTOVER'S PIZZA

INGREDIENTS

Leftover Turkey from Christmas dinner
Pizza bases (as many as you need)
Cranberry sauce
Leftover Turkey gravy
Brie cheese
Edam cheese, grated
Pistachio nuts, chopped

METHOD

Shred, pull or chop the turkey and toss it in a bit of gravy if you've got it. Arrange evenly across the pizza bread.

Slice the Brie, or pull apart with your fingers and arrange on top of pizza.

Sprinkle pistachios across the top. Spread a thin layer of Edam over. Grill or bake until the cheese melts and the base browns.

Remove from oven, add a whole lot of little dollops of cranberry sauce, then season with salt and pepper and serve!

Tip: You can do this with croissants or flat bread and for a thinner, healthier option try tortillas.

PREP TIME
10 minutes

COOK TIME
12 minutes

SERVES
2 per pizza

This pizza is a version of my favourite sandwich from Singapore , so credit must go to Project Blood Brothers Cafe for their chicken, cranberry and Brie open sandwich, with pistachios - *Sean*

SWEET

TREATS

Easy, quick, delicious,
if you've got heaps of bananas
just make more! - *Donna*

BANANA BREAD

INGREDIENTS

5+ mashed overripe bananas
2 cups all-purpose flour
2 eggs, beaten
¾ cup brown sugar

¾ tsp baking soda
½ cup butter
¼ tsp salt

METHOD

Preheat oven to 165°C.

Lightly grease a 9x5 inch loaf pan.

In a large bowl, combine flour, baking soda and salt.

In a separate bowl, cream together butter and brown sugar. Use a fork to stir eggs and mashed bananas until well blended.

Fold the banana mixture into flour mixture to a thick moist batter. Pour into a prepared loaf pan.

Bake in preheated fan bake oven for 55-60 minutes. Insert a toothpick/skewer to check if it's cooked. If it comes out clean - it's ready!

Let the banana bread cool in pan for 10 minutes, then turn out onto a wire rack.

Tip 1: This recipe doubles nicely and the more bananas the better. You can also add coconut for a bit more texture. AND you can freeze it! Slice it first, then you can pop a frozen slice into the toaster and have with a big dollop of butter.

Tip 2: Don't cream the butter and sugar for too long, just until it feels creamy and smooth. A.k.a properly mixed together!

PREP TIME
20 minutes

COOK TIME
45 minutes

SERVES
Family of 6

NAN'S CHOCOLATE

RUMBLE (A.K.A. JORDAN'S CRYPTONITE)

INGREDIENTS

5 crushed weetbix
2 cups all-purpose flour
1 cup desiccated coconut
2 tbsp cocoa
1 cup brown sugar
¾ tsp baking powder
250gms melted butter
Salt, pinch

BASIC CHOCOLATE ICING

1½ cups icing sugar
2 tbsp cocoa (heaped)
2 tbsp melted butter
Water, 1 tsp at a time

METHOD

Preheat oven to 165°C.

Lightly grease a loaf or slice pan with butter.

In a large bowl, combine all ingredients. Pour in melted butter, mix together (save a little coconut to sprinkle on the icing).

Press firmly into the loaf pan.

Bake in preheated fan bake oven for about 45 minutes.

Smother in chocolate icing and sprinkle with coconut OR spoon some into a bowl while hot and eat as dessert with ice cream.

Tip: Even though the loaf pan is greased, it's a good idea to line the dish with baking paper. It makes it easier to get the slice out of the tin.

If you have a wheat intolerance DO NOT EAT THIS! There's a reason it's also known as Jordan's cryptonite!

PREP TIME	COOK TIME	SERVES
20 minutes	*45 minutes*	*Family of 6*

Eat hot out of the oven. Top with vanilla
ice-cream and make sure someone is
around to hide it before
you've had your third helping - *Donna*

One of Nan's excellent
simple recipes that the kids like
to help with... especially
the eating part! - *Donna*

NAN'S FAMOUS

FRUIT CRUMBLE

INGREDIENTS

½ cup brown sugar (*any sugar works)
8 tbsp or 120g soft butter
¼ tsp salt
1 cup all-purpose flour
½ cup rolled oats
Cooked rhubarb, or feijoas
Apples, or pears

METHOD

Rub butter and sugar, salt, flour and oats together until crumbly. Get someone with cold fingers to do this, if your hands are hot you'll just melt the butter.

Taste test it... you might have to do this a few times.

Thinly slice apple or pear and lay across bottom of pan, sprinkle a little sugar and pour cooked feijoa or rhubarb on top. We've also added frozen or canned berries. It all works well.

Spoon a thick layer of crumble on top, gently press into corners.

Bake in preheated fan bake oven at 160°C for 40 minutes until the crumble is golden brown and the fruit is cooked. Another 10 minutes if you want more crunch.

Eat with vanilla ice cream, cream or yoghurt. You won't regret it!

Tip: Nan doesn't put oats in hers, but I prefer it with! Apple, rhubarb, feijoa, pear, berries any of these go great with it. This is a double mixture because a single mix is not enough!

PREP TIME	COOK TIME	SERVES
10 minutes	*40 minutes*	*Family of 6*

Sean has a saying:
"Food, like love -
should be a pleasure to make."

FOOD IS LOVE

www.ingramcontent.com/pod-product-compliance
Lightning Source LLC
Chambersburg PA
CBHW040316100426
42811CB00012B/1456